SandCastle
Let's Go!

LET'S GO
BY
BUS

ANDERS HANSON

Consulting Editor, Diane Craig, M.A./Reading Specialist

ABDO Publishing Company

Published by ABDO Publishing Company, 8000 West 78th Street, Edina, MN 55439.

Printed in the United States.

Editor: Pam Price
Curriculum Coordinator: Nancy Tuminelly
Cover and Interior Design and Production: Mighty Media
Photo Credits: JupiterImages Corporation, Shutterstock

Library of Congress Cataloging-in-Publication Data

Hanson, Anders, 1980-
    Let's go by bus / Anders Hanson.
        p. cm. -- (Let's go!)
    ISBN 978-1-59928-895-6
    1. Buses--Juvenile literature. 2. Bus travel--Juvenile literature. I. Title.

TL232.H373 2008
629.28'333--dc22

                                                                          2007006419

SandCastle™ Level: Transitional

SandCastle™ books are created by a team of professional educators, reading specialists, and content developers around five essential components—phonemic awareness, phonics, vocabulary, text comprehension, and fluency—to assist young readers as they develop reading skills and increase their general knowledge. All books are written, reviewed, and leveled for guided reading, early intervention reading, and Accelerated Reader® programs for use in shared, guided, and independent reading and writing activities to support a balanced approach to literacy instruction. The SandCastle™ series has four levels that correspond to early literacy development. The levels are provided to help teachers and parents select appropriate books for young readers.

Emerging Readers
(no flags)

Beginning Readers
(1 flag)

Transitional Readers
(2 flags)

Fluent Readers
(3 flags)

SandCastle™ would like to hear from you. Please send us your comments or questions.

sandcastle@abdopublishing.com

Buses can carry a lot of people and luggage from one place to another.

Buses have big tires.

5

The steering wheel turns the bus.

The driver uses the mirror to see beside the bus.

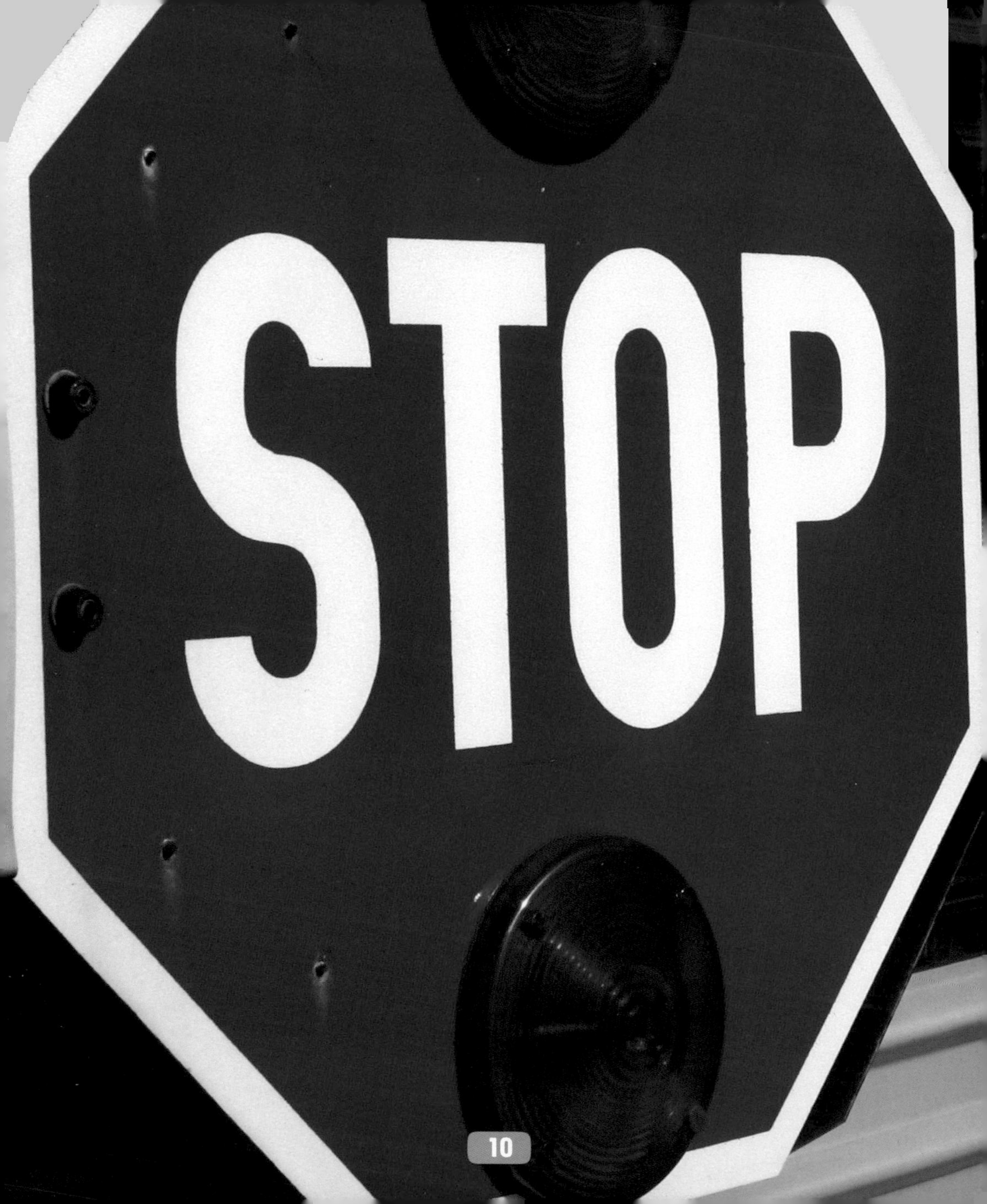
STOP

A stop sign helps kids cross the road safely.

Kayla and Janna
ride the bus
to school.

Mr. Jones is at the bus stop. He checks the schedule to see when the bus will come.

Peter takes a
bus to visit his
best friend.
His friend lives
in Chicago.

London is famous for its big, red double-decker buses.

HAVE YOU BEEN ON A BUS?

WHERE DID YOU GO?

TYPES OF BUSES

commuter bus

double-decker bus

minibus

motor coach

school bus

FAST FACTS

The word *bus* comes from the Latin word *omnibus,* which means "for all."

The first buses were created in Europe in the 1820s.

School buses have been the same yellow color since 1939. The color was chosen because black lettering is easy to read on a bright yellow background.

GLOSSARY

commuter – a person or vehicle that travels back and forth regularly.

luggage – suitcases or other containers for carrying a traveler's belongings.

minibus – a small bus or van.

mirror – a polished or smooth surface, such as glass, that reflects images.

schedule – a list of the times when things will happen.

To see a complete list of SandCastle™ books and other nonfiction titles from ABDO Publishing Company, visit **www.abdopublishing.com**.

8000 West 78th Street, Edina, MN 55439 • 800-800-1312 • 952-831-1632 fax